pinpoint ENGLISH
whole class reading

Flexible and Creative Lessons for

Boy in the Tower

by Polly Ho-Yen

Y6

Published by Pearson Education Limited, 80 Strand, London, WC2R 0RL.

www.pearsonschools.co.uk

Text © Pearson Education Limited 2019
Edited by Pearson Education Limited and Just Content Limited
Designed and typeset by Pearson Education Limited and PDQ Media
Original illustrations © Pearson Education Limited 2019
Illustrated by PDQ Media
Characters illustrated by The Boy Fitz Hammond
Cover design by Pearson Education Limited 2019
Cover illustration © Pearson Education Limited 2019

The right of Annabel Gray to be identified as author of this work has been asserted by her in accordance with the Copyright, Designs and Patents Act 1988.

First published 2019

22 21 20 19
10 9 8 7 6 5 4 3 2 1

British Library Cataloguing in Publication Data
A catalogue record for this book is available from the British Library

ISBN 978 1 292 27403 4

Copyright notice
All rights reserved. The material in this publication is copyright. Activity sheets may be freely photocopied for classroom use in the purchasing institution. However, this material is copyright and under no circumstances may copies be offered for sale. If you wish to use the material in any way other than that specified you must apply in writing to the publishers.

Printed in the UK by Ashford Press Ltd

Acknowledgements

P 61: 'Binley House' from *Overheard in a Tower Block*, copyright © 2017 Joseph Coelho

Note from the publisher
Pearson has robust editorial processes, including answer and fact checks, to ensure the accuracy of the content in this publication, and every effort is made to ensure that this publication is free of errors. We are, however, only human, and occasionally errors do occur. Pearson is not liable for any misunderstandings that arise as a result of errors in this publication, but it is our priority to ensure that the content is accurate. If you spot an error, please do contact us at resourcescorrections@pearson.com so we can make sure it is corrected.

Contents

Programme overview — 4

Using Whole Class Reading — 5

Activity planning guide — 6

Synopsis — 8

Starter activities — 9

Main activities — 23

Plenary activities — 38

Photocopiable masters — 49

Answers — 63

Programme overview

Introduction

Pinpoint English Whole Class Reading is your new go-to resource for flexible, high-quality activities based on the best children's books, with a strong focus on turning readers into writers and developing rich vocabularies.

Whole Class Reading is curriculum-matched, allowing you to target the skills required to ensure success in the national curriculum for English.

Principles

- As the teacher, you can choose which texts to teach in which order, matching with your focus topic for a particular week or term, the needs of your class or just your personal favourites.
- Each text has been chosen by an experienced panel of children's writers, librarians and teachers.
- The Whole Class Reading series allows you to rediscover classroom favourites as well as explore new titles that champion diversity and broaden your class's horizons.
- Activities provide opportunities to engage with fiction, poetry and non-fiction, with curriculum objectives provided for each task.
- Reading comprehension is taught through discussion and written activities, providing practice of essential skills.
- Spoken language skills are improved through lively debate, discussions and games.
- Vocabulary, spelling and grammar are taught in the context of a real writer's choices.
- Activities are differentiated where appropriate yet complementary so that the whole class can enjoy reading together.

Programme structure

- Whole Class Reading provides a vast, flexible range of starter, main and plenary activities to empower you to teach with confidence.
- Review the activities, pinpoint the skills you want to cover and build engaging lessons.
- Look out for differentiated activities to allow you to keep the whole class together.

 These tasks provide a low-threshold starting point to build the foundations of understanding.

 These tasks are pitched at age-related expectations so that children who can complete the work confidently and accurately display a firm grasp of the topic or skill.

 These tasks challenge children to explore the topic or skill in greater depth.

Using Whole Class Reading

Suggested activity timings are shown here. Some activities can be carried out over several lessons.

Resource lists let you know which photocopiable masters and materials you will need.

Milestones suggest how far you should read before carrying out the activity.

Vocabulary builder activities help children to expand their vocabularies.

Word puddle

READ UP TO PAGE 14

(10) (WORD) Vocabulary builder **Resources required:** plain paper

- **Children should be able to:**
  identify how language, structure and presentation contribute to meaning; identify and discuss themes and conventions in and across a wide range of writing.

1. Read pages 6–14 and ask children to think of one word to sum up the chapter. They may identify that 'rain' or 'water' is a theme that runs throughout.
2. Ask children to draw a large puddle on a page of A4 paper.
3. Challenge groups or pairs of children to find words in the chapter that link to rain and write them in their puddles. This activity could be run as a timed competition, e.g. see how many words they can find in three minutes.

(D) Children could be 'puddle monitors' and check that other groups have only included relevant words.

Starter activity 5

Each activity explores areas of the **national curriculum**.

Activities are pitched at the 'Securing' level. Where appropriate, you will find **differentiation ideas** here.

Curriculum areas covered in this title

- spoken language
- reading
- writing
- spelling, punctuation and grammar
- PSHE
- citizenship
- science
- computing
- design and technology
- geography
- art and design

Activity planning guide

The magic of Whole Class Reading is that you can mix and match activities in a way that works for you, your class and the time you can dedicate to *Boy in the Tower*. Sometimes, you might spend a whole lesson reading; at other times, you might build a structured lesson from the 90 activities you'll find in this book. Below is an overview of these activities, complete with reading milestones (in brackets) and pairing suggestions.

Starter activities

1: *Design and technology* (before reading)
Build the tallest tower and investigate its structure.
Works well with Main 1.

2: *Reading* (before reading)
Make predictions about the book.

3: *Speaking* (to page 5)
Ask questions about the intriguing first chapter.

4: *Geography; art* (to page 5)
Create aerial maps of Ade's neighbourhood.

5: *Vocabulary* (to page 14)
Create a rain word puddle.

6: *Grammar* (to page 58)
Use lists to write about characters in the book.

7: *Vocabulary* (to page 58)
Find synonyms for interesting words in the book.

8: *Vocabulary* (to page 94)
Find synonyms for interesting words in the book.

9: *Vocabulary* (to page 159)
Find synonyms for interesting words in the book.

10: *Vocabulary* (to page 222)
Find synonyms for interesting words in the book.

11: *Vocabulary* (to page 329)
Find synonyms for interesting words in the book.

12: *Drama* (to page 74)
Act out news interviews.

13: *Grammar* (to page 94)
Use semi-colons to join clauses.

14: *Reading* (to page 97)
Think about what is important to each of us.

Main activities

1: *Design and technology* (before reading)
Design and build a model of the book's front cover.
Works well with Starter 1.

2: *Vocabulary* (before reading)
Write similes about the view from the tower.

3: *Writing* (to page 16)
Write descriptively about the view from the tower.

4–5: *Writing* (to page 54)
Write a letter to Ade's mum.
This is a two-lesson mini-project.

6: *Reading* (to page 54)
Collect information about Ade and Gaia.

7: *Writing* (to page 89)
Write a diary entry, replicating the author's style.

8: *Speaking* (to page 97)
Debate Ade's next move.
Works well before Main 9.

9: *Writing* (to page 97)
Write a discussion text about Ade's next move.
Works well after Main 8.

10–11: *Writing* (to page 129)
Create non-fiction for a young audience.
This is a two-lesson mini-project.

12–13: *Science; writing* (to page 134)
Research carnivorous plants.
This is a two-lesson mini-project.
Works well before Main 14.

14: *Science* (to page 134)
Write about how the Bluchers have adapted to their environment.
Works well after Mains 12–13.

Plenary activities

1: *Reading* (before reading)
Think about real and fictional towers.

2: *Vocabulary* (before reading)
Play an expanded noun phrase memory game.

3: *Reading* (to page 5)
Find evidence to support a point of view.

4: *Art* (to page 5)
Sketch what a Blucher could look like.

5: *Reading* (to page 23)
Write a list of Ade's responsibilities.

6: *Citizenship* (to page 34)
Try lip-reading and think about how it might feel to be deaf.

7: *Writing* (to page 75)
Write effective news headlines.

8–10: *Reading* (during reading)
Compile a Blucher scrapbook.
This activity can be carried out as many times as you like. At least three times is recommended.

11: *Grammar* (to page 97)
Use the subjunctive to discuss a character's situation.

12: *Grammar* (to page 165)
Use the subjunctive to discuss a character's situation.

13: *Grammar* (to page 242)
Use the subjunctive to discuss a character's situation.

Starter activities	**Main activities**	**Plenary activities**

Starter activities

15: *Vocabulary* (to page 129)
Come up with definitions for new words from the book.

16: *Reading* (to page 147)
Investigate how tense can affect storytelling.

17: *Drama* (to page 222)
Create freeze frames to express characters' feelings.

18: *Drama* (to page 286)
Create freeze frames to express characters' feelings.

19: *Drama* (to page 329)
Create freeze frames to express characters' feelings.

20: *Reading* (after reading)
Separate fact from opinion.

21: *Speaking* (after reading)
Ask the big questions.

22: *Speaking* (after reading)
Reveal our predictions.

23: *Vocabulary* (after reading)
Work out the meaning of new vocabulary.

24: *Reading* (after reading)
Use comprehension questions to understand a text.

25: *Reading* (after reading)
Express opinions about a poem.

26: *Vocabulary* (after reading)
Learn the meaning of unfamiliar words in a poem.

27: *Reading* (after reading)
Express opinions about a poem.

28: *Reading* (after reading)
Perform a new poem.

29: *Vocabulary* (after reading)
Learn the meaning of unfamiliar words in a poem.

30: *Reading* (after reading)
Explore metaphor in poetry.

Main activities

15: *Reading* (to page 54)
Collect information about Dory and Gaia.

16–17: *Writing* (to page 169)
Create a 'how to survive the Bluchers' leaflet.
This is a two-lesson mini-project.

18–19: *Writing* (to page 182)
Write a letter from Ade to Gaia.
This is a two-lesson mini-project.

20: *Writing* (to page 246)
Write an extract from Ade's autobiography.

21: *Reading* (to page 322)
Order events as they appear in the book.

22: *Reading* (after reading)
Compare characters using antonyms.

23: *PSHE* (after reading)
Reflect on how the book has affected us personally.

24: *Reading* (after reading)
Review the book.

25: *Reading* (after reading)
Compare the Bluchers to Ade's mum's illness.

26: *Art* (after reading)
Create watercolour paintings of the Bluchers.

27–28: *Writing* (after reading)
Write a poem inspired by Binley House.
Works well with Plenary 28.

29–30: *Design and technology* (after reading)
Learn how to make origami cranes.

Plenary activities

14: *Vocabulary* (to page 94)
Ask the prime minister questions about the Blucher disaster.

15: *Reading* (to page 169)
Predict what happens next.

16: *Reading* (to page 94)
Decide whether each statement is true or false.

17: *Reading* (to page 222)
Decide whether each statement is true or false.

18: *Reading* (to page 329)
Decide whether each statement is true or false.

19: *Reading* (to page 222)
Play a guess who game.

20–22: *Reading* (after reading)
Draw a rollercoaster of emotions for Ade, Ben and Dory.
This is a three-lesson mini-project.

23: *Reading* (after reading)
Ask "why?".

24: *Geography* (after reading)
Mark the Blucher 'safe zones' on a map.

25: *Grammar* (after reading)
Explore the active and passive voices.

26: *Grammar* (after reading)
Understand how hyphens can clarify meaning.

27: *Reading* (after reading)
Answer questions as the poet.

28: *Reading* (after reading)
Explore metaphor in poetry.

29–30: *Reading* (after reading)
Learn a poem by heart and perform it to the class.

Synopsis

Boy in the Tower by Polly Ho-Yen

Ade loves living on the seventeenth floor of his tower block, watching the world beneath his window and spending time at school with his best friend, Gaia. But after a period of heavy rain, strange things start happening: buildings are falling and people are collapsing but no one knows why.

Curious, menacing plants begin to appear, putting everyone at risk. The community starts to flee to safety but Ade, whose sick mum hasn't left the house in months, is trapped in his tower block, seemingly alone.

With the Bluchers taking over and the deadly spores preventing search and rescue, things look bleak for Ade and his mum, until he discovers Dory and Obi, the only other remaining residents of his block.

Together, they enjoy an unlikely friendship filled with hot suppers, survival and hope, and embark on dangerous missions, such as Obi's trip to Gaia's tower and Ade's ill-advised rescue of a local cat.

An emotional finale sees the adults in the story sacrifice themselves for Ade. However, at the last minute, help arrives in a helicopter. The characters are saved and taken to safety. The story ends at the seaside, where Ade is reunited with Gaia.

About the author

Polly Ho-Yen is a writer from Bristol. After working in publishing and as a primary school teacher, Polly was inspired to write stories about the communities that she met.

Boy in the Tower was her debut novel and was shortlisted for the Blue Peter Book Award, Waterstones Children's Book Prize and the Federation of Children's Book Groups Book Award.

Polly now runs writing workshops in primary and secondary schools across the country, as well as working for Bristol libraries.

Starter activities

Towers — BEFORE READING

⏱ **Resources required:** blocks, cubes, tins, or anything else that children could use to build a tower

- **Children should be able to:**
  select from and use a wider range of materials and components, including construction materials, textiles and ingredients, according to their functional properties and aesthetic qualities.

1 Set out the range of building materials for children to choose from.
2 Without linking this to the story, challenge children in small groups to make a tower as tall as possible using any of the materials.
3 Discuss which towers are the strongest, and why.
4 Explain that children will be reading a book about a tower and reveal the front cover.

This activity could be extended into a main task with a deeper focus on planning, design and functionality.

Starter activity 1

Keep a secret — BEFORE READING

⏱ **Resources required:** one small piece of paper per child

- **Children should be able to:**
  predict what might happen from details stated and implied.

1 Look at the front cover together. Without discussing it, children make individual predictions about the book. Encourage children to think about characters and storyline, using evidence from the picture, title and the strapline. They could also think about what genre the book may belong to.
2 Children write their predictions on small pieces of paper and fold them up without showing them to anyone else.
3 Put the predictions in a safe place, ready to open when they have finished the book.

ⓓ Ask children to practise writing succinctly by writing their predictions as blurbs of no more than 30 words.

Starter activity 2

Before

⏱ 10 **Resources required:** sticky notes

- **Children should be able to:**

  participate in discussions.

  ask questions to improve their understanding of a text.

1 Read pages 3–5 aloud to the class.

2 Choose some sentences and ask children what questions they raise, e.g. Why does the character wish it was Monday? What are the Bluchers? What has changed about the view? Where is Gaia?

3 Collect the questions on sticky notes and display in the classroom. These can be answered as the class progresses through the book.

4 Ask children to consider why they think the author leaves so many questions unanswered in the first chapter.

D Some children may want to predict the answers to questions using evidence from the text: I think Gaia is the narrator's friend because he can always recognise her.

Starter activity 3

The view from above

READ UP TO PAGE 5

⏱ 15 **Resources required:** plain paper, aerial map (T only)

- **Children should be able to:**

  check that the book makes sense to them, discussing their understanding.

  use fieldwork to observe, measure, record and present the human and physical features in the local area using a range of methods, including sketch maps, plans and graphs, and digital technologies.

  improve their mastery of art and design techniques, including drawing, painting and sculpture with a range of materials [for example, pencil, charcoal, paint, clay].

1 Ask children to discuss times when they have seen an aerial view of an area, e.g. from an aeroplane or a tall building. If possible, take the class to view the ground from above and notice how the perspective changes.

2 Ask children to make a note of all the features that Ade can see from his towerblock.

3 Children create an aerial map of what they think Ade can see out of his window.

T If children struggle, show them an example of an aerial map or provide them with a list of the features mentioned in the book.

Starter activity 4

Word puddle

 Vocabulary builder **Resources required:** plain paper

- **Children should be able to:**
  identify how language, structure and presentation contribute to meaning; identify and discuss themes and conventions in and across a wide range of writing.

1. Read pages 6–14 and ask children to think of one word to sum up the chapter. They may identify that 'rain' or 'water' is a theme that runs throughout.
2. Ask children to draw a large puddle on a page of A4 paper.
3. Challenge groups or pairs of children to find words in the chapter that link to rain and write them in their puddles. This activity could be run as a timed competition, e.g. see how many words they can find in three minutes.

Children could be 'puddle monitors' and check that other groups have only included relevant words.

Starter activity 5

Character bullet points

- **Children should be able to:**

 ask questions to improve their understanding.

 punctuate bullet points consistently.

1. Ask children to think about the three main characters that they have met so far (Ade, Gaia and Ade's mum).
2. Using bullet points, ask them to list two facts about each character and one question that they still have about the character, e.g. Will Ade's mum get better? Why will Ade lose Gaia?

You may want to model how to use bullet points, i.e. consistent use of capital letters and full stops.

Starter activity 6

Synonyms

 DURING READING

5 x 10 **Vocabulary builder Resources required:** thesauruses (T only)

- **Children should be able to:**

   learn how words are related by meaning as synonyms.

  check that the book makes sense to them, discussing their understanding and exploring the meaning of words in context.

1 This activity can be carried out at various points during reading.

2 Ask children to find synonyms for the words below. Remind children that a synonym is a word that means the same, or nearly the same, as another word.

3 You could ask children to write down the words in their books, or you could write each list on the board once you have finished each of the sections.

Pages 3–58:
- murky (page 7)
- sodden (page 11)
- dangerous (page 21)
- bizarre (page 33)
- shoved (page 52)

Pages 59–94
- scared (page 61)
- collapsed (page 63)
- examining (page 73)
- abandoned (page 74)
- menacing (page 86)

Pages 95–159:
- nervous (page 100)
- disaster (page 108)
- desperately (page 124)
- peering (page 146)
- teeter (page 153)

Pages 160–222:
- surrounded (page 160)
- thoughtfully (page 165)
- lonely (page 182)
- shimmers (page 206)
- cumbersome (page 214)

Pages 223–329:
- obviously (page 224)
- succulent (page 257)
- startled (page 262)
- swirling (page 273)
- creeping (page 292)

T Children could use thesauruses to support them.

D Children could be given just the chapter number and have to skim and scan to locate the words themselves.

Starter activities 7–11

Newsreaders

- **Children should be able to:**
  participate in discussions, presentations, performances, role play, improvisations and debates; select and use appropriate registers for effective communication.

1 Using pages 73 and 74, children take on the roles of the newsreader, Kathy, and the reporter, Bill.
2 In pairs, they practise being newsreaders, using the text as a script. Encourage children to use their voices to convey urgency and gravity.
3 Each group performs to the class. Other groups feed back on whether the performance was believable, and if not, how to make it more so.

Starter activity 12

Making connections

 Resources required: photocopy master (PCM) 1, scissors

- **Children should be able to:**
  use the semi-colon, colon and dash to mark the boundary between independent clauses.

1 Remind children that semi-colons separate two main clauses of equal importance.
2 Using PCM 1, children cut out and match the closely related clauses and separate them using a semi-colon.

Some children could write their own clauses using semi-colons accurately.

Starter activity 13

Leaving the tower

- **Children should be able to:**
  articulate and justify answers, arguments and opinions.

1 Read pages 95–97 as a class.
2 Ask children to think what they would take if they had to leave their home in a rush. Encourage children to articulate their reasons for the items that they choose.
3 Children list ten items that they would take on a piece of paper, then whittle these down to five and finally choose one item as the most important.

In pairs, children could be challenged to convince their partner to change their mind about an item and to swap it for another.

Starter activity 14

New words

 Vocabulary builder

READ UP TO PAGE 129

- **Children should be able to:**
  check that the book makes sense to them, discussing their understanding and exploring the meaning of words in context.

1 Read pages 119–129 as a class.
2 In pairs, ask children to explain the following vocabulary to each other.
   - Bluchers (page 121)
   - species (page 122)
   - swelling (page 123)
   - dissolve (page 123)
3 Ask for volunteers to repeat their partners' definitions to the class, if they feel they are particularly effective.

Starter activity 15

Before and now

READ UP TO PAGE 147

- **Children should be able to:**
  identify how language, structure and presentation contribute to meaning.

1 Ask children to read one paragraph on page 24, followed by one paragraph on page 147. Do they notice something different about the styles of writing? (Page 24 is written in the past tense and page 147 is written in the present tense.) Consider why this might be.
2 Ask children to collect ten examples of verbs in the past tense from pages 24–34 and ten examples of verbs in the present tense from pages 147–150.

 Challenge some children to scan the pages to find the same verb in different tenses, e.g. *was / is* or *said / say*, placing them into lists by tense.

Starter activity 16

Feelings freeze frames

3 x **Resources required:** hall or large space

- **Children should be able to:**

 draw inferences such as inferring characters' feelings, thoughts and motives from their actions, and justify inferences with evidence.

participate in discussions, presentations, performances, role play, improvisations and debates.

1 Children walk around a clear space. Call out a statement, give some thinking time and then clap your hands.
2 When children hear the clap, they freeze in a position that shows the character and the situation that has been called out.
3 While children are frozen in position, tap some children on the shoulder who can then 'come to life' and say what the character is thinking.

Pages 139–222:
- Ade is dehydrated.
- Ade discovers the water.
- Obi goes to Gaia's towerblock.
- Ade's mum smashes plates.
- Ben talks about Evie.

Pages 223–286:
- Ade notices a flicker of movement in the bushes.
- Ade is caught by the Blucher.
- Obi saves Ade from the Blucher.
- Dori catches pigeons.
- Ade's mum gets up.

Pages 287–329:
- Ade hears the rain.
- Ade realises he has to save himself and leave the others behind.
- Ade's mum stops at the door onto the roof.
- Obi jumps from the falling tower.
- Ade walks home with Gaia in their new town.

Starter activities 17–19

Fact or opinion?

 Resources required: two sheets of paper (write 'fact', on one and 'opinion' on the other)

- **Children should be able to:**

 distinguish between statements of fact and opinion.

1 Place the sign saying 'fact' on one side of the room and the sign saying 'opinion' on the other side of the room.

2 Read out the following statements.
   - *Boy in the Tower* is a great book.
   - The characters end up in a safe zone.
   - Obi is the hero of the story.
   - The author is Polly Ho-Yen.
   - The Bluchers are evil.
   - Ade lives on the 17th floor.

3 For each statement, children move towards the 'fact' or 'opinion' side of the room, depending on what they think. Ask children to explain their decision.

4 Reveal the correct answer and ensure that any children standing by the wrong sign understand why the statement is fact or opinion.

Children ask themselves: is it true? (fact); is it what somebody thinks? (opinion)

Children suggest statements for the class to decide on. Make sure they know the answer themselves.

Starter activity 20

Big questions

- **Children should be able to:**

 ask relevant questions to extend their understanding and knowledge.

 ask questions to improve their understanding.

1 Children think of important questions they have about the book. They could be questions for the characters, for the author, for you – or even for themselves.

2 In groups, ask children to choose their most pressing question now that they have finished the book. What are they dying to find out?

3 Collect these on the board and leave them there for the rest of the session, or the whole day if possible.

Encourage children to think about the big questions relating to the plot, e.g. Which is more powerful: humans or nature? Why is it important to look after those who are more in need of help than ourselves?

Encourage children to think about the deeper questions, e.g. What did Ade learn? How have the characters' relationships changed over the course of the story?

Starter activity 21

Revealing our secrets

 Resources required: children's predictions from Starter activity 2

- **Children should be able to:**

  articulate and justify answers, arguments and opinions.

1 Hand out the original predictions that children made from Starter activity 2 so that each child gets one (not their own).
2 Children open and read the predictions to the class.
3 Give the children five minutes to stand in a line, ordering the predictions from most accurate to least accurate.

Starter activity 22

Non-fiction: glossary

 **Vocabulary builder Resources required:** photocopy master (PCM) 8, dictionaries

- **Children should be able to:**

   apply their growing knowledge of root words, prefixes and suffixes (morphology and etymology), as listed in English Appendix 1, both to read aloud and to understand the meaning of new words that they meet.

   use the first three or four letters of a word to check spelling, meaning or both of these in a dictionary.

1 Children can do this activity at any time.
2 Ask children to read PCM 8. Then ask them to read out the words in bold for you to write on the whiteboard.
3 In pairs, ask children to discuss and note down what the words could mean, based on the context, their comprehension of the book and their knowledge of root words, prefixes and suffixes.
4 Children check the meaning of the words in a dictionary or with other members of the class and design their own glossary to accompany the text.

Children could find synonyms for each new word.

Starter activity 23

Non-fiction: quick comprehension

Resources required: photocopy masters (PCM) 8 and 9

- **Children should be able to:**

  summarise the main ideas drawn from more than one paragraph, identifying key details that support the main ideas; retrieve and record information from non-fiction.

1 Ask children to get into groups of three and find a place in the classroom to work. Hand out PCM 9 to each group.

2 Place copies of PCM 8 in different locations around the room. One at a time, children must read a question on PCM 9, walk to wherever PCM 8 is displayed, find the answer and take it back to their group to note down. Repeat for all questions.

Ask children to take a pencil and paper to make notes as they look for the answers.

This could be run as a competition with the fastest group winning.

Starter activity 24

Poetry: *Bluchers* opinions

Resources required: photocopy master (PCM) 12, A3 paper, sticky notes

- **Children should be able to:**

  participate in discussions about books that are read to them and those they can read for themselves, building on their own and others' ideas and challenging views courteously; provide reasoned justifications for their views.

  listen and respond appropriately to adults and their peers.

1 Write these statements on pieces of A3 paper and place on tables with copies of the poem (PCM 12).

   - The poem uses alliteration.
   - The poet likes the Bluchers.
   - Bluchers are dangerous.
   - The poem does not use repetition.
   - The poem could be written by Ade.
   - The poem uses the passive voice.

2 In groups, children move to each table. They have one minute to decide if they collectively agree or disagree with the statement. They write 'agree' or 'disagree' on a sticky note and put it on the paper.

3 Discuss each statement, taking into account differing points of view. Ask children to use evidence from the poem.

This activity is intended for children working at the 'towards level' but can be differentiated as shown.

Ask children to undertake the activity independently.

Children could write down their evidence with line references and explanations.

Starter activity 25

Poetry: *Bluchers* vocabulary

 Vocabulary builder **Resources required:** photocopy master (PCM) 12, dictionaries, thesauruses

- **Children should be able to:**

   apply their growing knowledge of root words, prefixes and suffixes (morphology and etymology), as listed in English Appendix 1, both to read aloud and to understand the meaning of new words that they meet.

   use the first three or four letters of a word to check spelling, meaning or both of these in a dictionary.

1. Ask children to read the poem (PCM 12) and underline any unfamiliar words.
2. In partners, children discuss and note down what the words could mean.
3. Children check the meaning of the words in a dictionary.

T This activity is intended for children working at the 'towards level' but can be differentiated as shown.

S Ask children to make a glossary of their words so that they can use them in their own writing later.

D Ask children to use a thesaurus to find synonyms for each new word.

Starter activity 26

Poetry: *Binley House* opinions

Resources required: photocopy master (PCM) 13, A3 paper, sticky notes

- **Children should be able to:**

   participate in discussions about books that are read to them and those they can read for themselves, building on their own and others' ideas and challenging views courteously; provide reasoned justifications for their views.

   listen and respond appropriately to adults and their peers.

1 Write these statements on pieces of A3 paper and place on tables with copies of the poem (PCM 13).

- Binley House is quiet.
- Binley House is like Ade's towerblock.
- The poem rhymes.
- The poem uses similes and metaphors.
- The poet has lived in Binley House.
- The poem uses repetition.

2 In groups, children move to each table. They have one minute to decide if they collectively agree or disagree with the statement. They write 'agree' or 'disagree' on a sticky note and put it on the paper.

3 Discuss each statement, taking into account differing points of view. Ask children to use evidence from the poem.

T Read the poem to children, ensuring that your intonation matches the poem's tone.

S This activity is intended for children working at the 'securing level' but can be differentiated as shown.

D Ask children to support others in making a decision.

Starter activity 27

Poetry: *Binley House* performance — AFTER READING

(15) Resources required: photocopy master (PCM) 13

- **Children should be able to:**
  - prepare poems and plays to read aloud and to perform, showing understanding through intonation, tone and volume so that the meaning is clear to an audience.
  - speak audibly and fluently with an increasing command of Standard English.

1. In small groups, children practise reading the poem (PCM 13) aloud, ensuring that they are audible and fluent.
2. Groups can decide how they want to deliver the poem so that it gets the message across.

T Children could read as a pair and have more time to practise before performing to the class.

S This activity is intended for children working at the 'securing level' but can be differentiated as shown.

D Children could take on the role of director, guiding others in delivering their lines.

Starter activity 28

Poetry: *Hope* vocabulary — AFTER READING

(10) Vocabulary builder **Resources required:** photocopy master (PCM) 14, dictionaries

- **Children should be able to:**
  - apply their growing knowledge of root words, prefixes and suffixes (morphology and etymology), as listed in English Appendix 1, both to read aloud and to understand the meaning of new words that they meet.
  - use the first three or four letters of a word to check spelling, meaning or both of these in a dictionary.

1. Ask children to read the poem (PCM 14) and underline any unfamiliar vocabulary.
2. In partners, children discuss and note down what the words could mean, based on context and their knowledge of root words, prefixes and suffixes.
3. Children check the meaning of the words in a dictionary.

T Children could be given the definitions to match up with the words.

S Remind children what root words, prefixes and suffixes are, and point out some examples within the text, e.g. sweetest, chillest, strangest. Can they find the root word? Does that help them to work out the meaning?

D This activity is intended for children working at the 'deeper level' but can be differentiated as shown.

Starter activity 29

Poetry: *Hope* metaphors

 Resources required: photocopy master (PCM) 14

- **Children should be able to:**

  understand the technical and other terms needed for discussing what they hear and read, such as metaphor, simile, analogy, imagery, style and effect; discuss and evaluate how authors use language, including figurative language, considering the impact on the reader.

1 Ask children to read the poem (PCM 14) aloud in pairs.

2 Ask: How does Emily Dickinson compare 'hope' to a bird? Children find examples of metaphors in the poem to support their ideas.

3 Ask: How do the characters in *Boy in the Tower* keep hope?

(T) Read the poem out loud, emphasising each metaphor.

(S) Ask children to start by highlighting individual words that remind them of a bird, before expanding their search to look for the whole metaphor.

(D) This activity is intended for children working at the 'deeper level' but can be differentiated as shown.

Starter activity 30

Main activities

Making a towerblock

 Resources required: cardboard boxes, paper, scissors, pens, paints; photocopy master (PCM) 13 (optional)

- **Children should be able to:**

   select from and use a wider range of materials and components according to their functional properties and aesthetic qualities; apply their understanding of how to strengthen, stiffen and reinforce more complex structures.

1 Write the word 'towerblock' on the board and ask children what they think a towerblock is. Discuss why towerblocks are often found in busy urban areas.

2 You might like to read the poem *Binley House* (PCM 13) to help children to understand what a towerblock is.

Using the front cover of the book as inspiration, ask children to design and make a model of a towerblock in groups. Ask them to consider:

- what material they will make it out of
- how they will show the floors (at least 17) and windows
- how they will show the balconies
- how they will show the boy and the light on the 17th floor.

3 Come back together as a class so that children can share their models with other groups. Ask the class to say three positive things about each model.

(T) Work in mixed ability groups so that children can support each other.

(D) Children could consider how the size of the tower might affect its stability.

Main activity 1

High-up similes

 Vocabulary builder **Resources required:** satellite view of urban area

- **Children should be able to:**

   understand the technical and other terms needed for discussing what they hear and read, such as metaphor, simile, analogy, imagery, style and effect.

   draft and write by describing settings, characters and atmosphere.

1 Show children a satellite view of an urban area and list what they can see.

2 Display the phrase 'people like ants' and ask children which literary device this is.

3 Model how to use similes to describe a scene, e.g. 'cars look like matchboxes, houses look like rows of teeth.' Ask children to write more similes about the scene.

(T) Children could have picture prompts to help with ideas for their similes.

(D) Children could be challenged to write metaphors as well as similes.

Main activity 2

Looking down

⏱ 50

- **Children should be able to:**

  write for a range of real purposes; select appropriate grammar and vocabulary; note and develop initial ideas, drawing on reading and research where necessary; ensure the consistent and correct use of tense throughout a piece of writing.

1. On pages 15–16, Ade describes what he can see from his window.

2. Children write a description of what they might be able to see from a towerblock window, adding detail by using imaginative vocabulary and literary devices. Children could draw on the ideas from Main activity 2, if completed.

3. Ask children to pay close attention to the tense they are using and ensure that they stay in that tense, e.g. Ade writes in the past tense ('I could always see …').

T Children may find it easier to write in the present tense, e.g. 'I can see …'.

D Children could be challenged to use two tenses for effect: before and after an event, for example.

Children may benefit from you modelling the opening of the description.

Main activity 3

Ade's mum

2 × ⏱ 40 **Resources required:** photocopy master (PCM) 2

- **Children should be able to:**

  draw inferences such as inferring characters' feelings, thoughts and motives from their actions, and justify inferences with evidence.

  plan their writing by noting and developing initial ideas, drawing on reading and research where necessary.

1. On page 19, Ade says that his mum is not like other mums. In the first session, ask children to find evidence to support this statement and collect on either an individual or a class mind map.

2. Using PCM 2, children plan a letter from Ade to his mum to persuade her to come to the shop. Children should draw on their knowledge and inferences of Ade's mum's situation and Ade's feelings about it.

3. In the second session, give children 40 minutes to write their letter.

T Children could write a note rather than a letter, focusing on the sentence stems:

   I worry …; I wish …; I hope …

D Children could also write a response from Ade's mum, addressing his concerns.

This topic could be difficult for some children, so ensure that it is tackled sensitively.

Main activities 4–5

Best friends

⏱ 40 **Resources required:** photocopy master (PCM) 3

- **Children should be able to:**

  summarise the main ideas drawn from more than one paragraph, identifying key details that support the main ideas.

1. Ask children to consider what they know about Ade and Gaia so far.
2. Children use PCM 3 to collect information on the characters in order to build a picture of them. They should write information about each character inside his or her outline and information about their relationships around the outside.
3. Invite children to share their information with the class to make sure everyone has a complete picture of each character. If a child is missing some information, they can add it to their PCM.

(T) Children may concentrate on one character.

(D) Children could write a comparative paragraph about the characters, discussing their similarities and differences.

Main activity 6

Dear diary

 45

- **Children should be able to:**

  write for a range of real purposes; select appropriate grammar and vocabulary; note and develop initial ideas, drawing on reading and research where necessary; use paragraphs to organise ideas around a theme; identify how language, structure and presentation contribute to meaning.

1. Read pages 87–89, asking children to recognise the techniques that the author has used to create suspense. This may include use of:
   - short sentences
   - repetition
   - onomatopoeia
   - rhetorical questions
   - powerful verbs.
2. Remind children of a diary's key features.
3. Children write their own diary entry as Ade, trying out some of the techniques that Polly Ho-Yen has used to create tension.

(T) Ask children to write one paragraph, focusing on one or two of the techniques. Remind children to check that they have used punctuation accurately.

(D) Ask children to explain to others how the techniques affect the reader.

Main activity 7

25

Class debate

 40

- **Children should be able to:**

   explain and discuss their understanding of what they have read, including through formal presentations and debates, maintaining a focus on the topic and using notes where necessary; participate in discussions about books building on their own and others' ideas and challenging views courteously.

   articulate and justify answers, arguments and opinions.

1 Display the following quote from page 97: 'I knew it was a good idea to get out, but the problem was, I just couldn't go anywhere without Mum.'

2 Ask the question: Should Ade leave the tower?

3 Ask children to stand on one side of the room if they think 'yes' and on the other side if they think 'no'. Ask children on each side of the debate to give reasons for their opinions.

4 After each person has spoken, allow children to decide if they have been persuaded to change their mind and would like to move to the other side.

(T) Ask children to write down some ideas to prepare for the debate.

(S) Ask children to note down some of the debate phrases to use in Main activity 9.

(D) Ask children to challenge views courteously, e.g. "I understand your point of view but I believe …"

This activity can be used as preparation for Main activity 9.

Main activity 8

Discussion text

READ UP TO PAGE 97

Resources required: any phrases collected in Main activity 8, photocopy master (PCM) 4

- **Children should be able to:**

 use a wide range of devices to build cohesion within and across paragraphs; proofread for spelling and punctuation errors.

 articulate and justify answers, arguments and opinions.

 use commas to clarify meaning or avoid ambiguity; use devices to build cohesion within a paragraph.

1 If you held the debate in Main activity 8, remind children of the arguments collected. If not, hold a five-minute discussion about the arguments for and against the question: Should Ade leave the tower?

2 Tell the class that they are now going to write a discussion piece about whether or not Ade should leave the tower. Model how to structure a discussion text using PCM 4 as a structural guide.

3 Encourage children to proofread their own and each other's work for spelling and punctuation errors.

T Ask children to focus on organising their writing into paragraphs: one paragraph per reason for or against.

S Ask children to use conjunctions to link their ideas.

D Ask children to use four alternating paragraphs, moving between for and against, and more complex conjunctions, such as: although, however, despite this, on the other hand.

This activity works well after Main activity 8.

Main activity 9

Non-fiction: changing the style

2 x 50 **Resources required:** photocopy master (PCM) 8, plain paper, markers

- **Children should be able to:**

 write for a range of real purposes; select appropriate grammar and vocabulary; note and develop initial ideas, drawing on reading and research where necessary; identify how language, structure, and presentation contribute to meaning; use further organisational and presentational devices to structure text and to guide the reader.

 recognise the difference between vocabulary typical of informal speech and vocabulary appropriate for formal speech and writing.

1. In the first session, explain that children will be writing and designing a leaflet that will get the message from PCM 8 across to younger members of the public. Ask them to plan their leaflet in pairs.

2. Suggest to them that, by thinking about why PCM 8 isn't suitable for younger children, they might be able to work out how to adapt it appropriately.

3. In the second session, they will design and make their leaflet.

4. They will need to consider:
   - how to use vocabulary that younger children will understand
   - how to use pictures to illustrate their points
   - how to ensure that children are not frightened by what they read.

Main activities 10–11

Carnivorous plants mini-project

2 x 50 **Resources required:** information texts about plants, access to the internet, paper, coloured pencils

- **Children should be able to:**

  note and develop initial ideas, drawing on reading and research where necessary.

  participate in discussions, presentations, performances, role play, improvisations and debates.

  retrieve, record and present information from non-fiction.

  give reasons for classifying plants and animals based on specific characteristics.

  use search technologies effectively, appreciate how results are selected and ranked, and be discerning in evaluating digital content.

1. Ask the children to use factual texts and the internet to make notes and plan for an information text about carnivorous plants. It may be helpful to model searching for information so that children understand how to decide whether the information is relevant.

2. Encourage children to collect information under the following headings.
   - What a carnivorous plant is
   - The different types of carnivorous plants
   - Where carnivorous plants are found
   - What carnivorous plants look like

3. During the second session, ask children to write their information text, using these headings and including images, diagrams and maps as appropriate.

   D Ask children to write their own headings to organise their work. They could be wide-ranging or focused on a specific plant.

Children may benefit from watching a film about carnivorous plants.

Main activities 12–13

Adaptation explanation

Resources required: photocopy master (PCM) 5

- **Children should be able to:**

   identify how animals and plants are adapted to suit their environment in different ways and that adaptation may lead to evolution.

1. Give out PCM 5 and ask children to consider how carnivorous plants have adapted over time in order to survive.
2. The Bluchers ate concrete, stone, glass and metal. Ask children to write their own short explanations of how and why the fictional Bluchers have adapted to their environment.

   Children could replicate the structure of the explanation on PCM 5.

   Ask children to draw their own diagrams to support their explanations.

This activity is best carried out after Main activities 12–13.

Main activity 14

New friends

Resources required: photocopy master (PCM) 6

- **Children should be able to:**

   summarise the main ideas drawn from more than one paragraph, identifying key details that support the main ideas.

1. Ask children to consider what they know about Dory and Obi so far.
2. Children use PCM 6 to collect information on the characters in order to build a picture of them. They should write information about each character inside his or her outline and information about their relationships around the outside.
3. Invite children to share their information with the class to make sure that everyone has a complete picture of each character. If a child is missing some information, they can add it to their PCM.

    Children may concentrate on one character.

   Children could write a comparative paragraph about the characters, discussing their similarities and differences.

Main activity 15

How to survive the Bluchers

READ UP TO PAGE 169

2 x 50 **Resources required:** paper and pens

- **Children should be able to:**

  use further organisational and presentational devices to structure text and to guide the reader [for example, headings, bullet points, underlining].

1 After reading pages 168–169, ask children to work in pairs to note down things a person must do to survive if they have to go outside with the Bluchers.

2 In the first session, children write their instructions. Remind them to make these as clear as possible, and use numbered steps to ensure that the reader can follow the instructions easily.

3 In the second session, children make a leaflet that could be handed out to members of the public. Discuss some key features of leaflets that may be helpful: headings, bullet-pointed lists, diagrams or images.

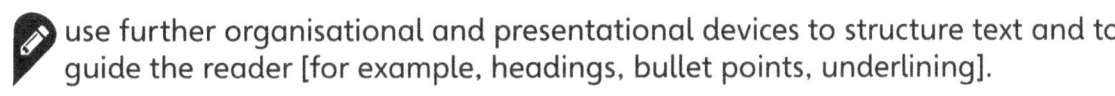

Main activities 16–17

A letter to Gaia

READ UP TO PAGE 182

2 x 50 **Resources required:** envelopes

- **Children should be able to:**

  note and develop initial ideas, drawing on reading and research where necessary; use paragraphs to organise ideas around a theme.

  recognise vocabulary and structures that are appropriate for formal speech and writing, including subjunctive forms.

1 In the first session, ask children how Ade might have felt when he heard that Gaia's tower had fallen. Discuss what Ade might have wanted to tell Gaia about what had happened since she left. Collect ideas on the board.

2 Children plan their letter from Ade to Gaia.

3 In the second session, ask children to write their letter. Remind them that Ade and Gaia are best friends so their letters to each other would be informal. Encourage children to use vocabulary specific to the story, including new words that Ade has learned. They may want to include the following ideas:

- what has been happening in Ade's tower
- what the Bluchers are doing
- Ade's new friends
- Ade's hopes and wishes.

4 Put their finished letters in envelopes to address, decorate and display.

T Ask children to focus on describing the tower setting and his new friends.

S Ask children to think about how Ade would speak in a letter to Gaia: he would probably use contractions and refer to their earlier shared experiences.

D Ask children to write a letter to Gaia's mother instead, taking into account how this difference in audience will affect the tone of their writing.

Main activities 18–19

Writing autobiographies

READ UP TO PAGE **246**

- **Children should be able to:**
  write for a range of real purposes; select appropriate grammar and vocabulary; note and develop initial ideas, drawing on reading and research where necessary; use paragraphs to organise ideas around a theme; identify how language, structure and presentation contribute to meaning.

1. Read pages 243–246, reminding children of the techniques the author has used to create suspense. This may include use of:
   - short sentences
   - repetition
   - onomatopoeia
   - rhetorical questions
   - powerful verbs.

2. Remind children of the features of an autobiography: they are written in the first person; they are factual; they are written in a narrative way, like stories. Have the children read any autobiographies? What did they like about them?

3. Tell children that they are going to write an extract from Ade's autobiography. The extract should cover the events on pages 243–246. Children should try out some of the techniques that Polly Ho-Yen has used to create tension.

T Ask children to write one paragraph, focusing on one or two of the techniques. Remind children to check that they have used punctuation accurately.

D Ask children to explain to others how the techniques affect the reader.

Main activity 20

The ending

READ UP TO PAGE **322**

 Resources required: photocopy master (PCM) 7, scissors

- **Children should be able to:**
   summarise the main ideas drawn from more than one paragraph.

1. Give out PCM 7 and ask children to cut up the sentences.
2. Using the text, children put the events in the order they occur in the book by arranging them on their desks.
3. Discuss the outcomes as a class.

Main activity 21

Compare the characters

⏱ 30 **Resources required:** string (roughly 2m), sticky notes

- **Children should be able to:**

 draw inferences such as inferring characters' feelings, thoughts and motives from their actions, and justify inferences with evidence.

 articulate and justify answers, arguments and opinions.

 learn how words are related by meaning as synonyms.

1 Write the names of the following characters on separate sticky notes: Ade; Dory; Obi; Ade's mum; Ben. Then write the following antonyms on separate sticky notes: strongest, weakest; kindest, meanest; happiest, saddest.

2 Ask two children to hold the string at the front of the class. Give them opposite words to hold up (e.g. 'strongest' at one end and 'weakest' at the other).

3 Give out the character sticky notes at random and ask those children to stand on the continuum line in order from strongest to weakest. Ask for textual evidence.

4 Ask the rest of the class to say whether they think any of the characters should move and why. Repeat with the other antonyms and with different children.

Ⓓ Ask children to think of other antonyms relevant to the characters in the book.

Encourage children to record ideas in written form if there is time.

Main activity 22

Personal reflections

⏱ 40

- **Children should be able to:**

 explain and discuss their understanding of what they have read.

 recognise and talk about their emotions, including having a varied vocabulary of words to use when talking about their own and others' feelings.

1 Tell children that they will be reflecting on how the book has affected them personally by writing answers to a series of questions and including evidence from the text. Explain that their answers will be kept private (unless they would like to share) and that it is likely that everyone will have different answers.

2 Children consider the whole text when writing responses to the following questions.

- What has the book taught you about friendship?
- What has the book taught you about surviving difficult circumstances?
- What has the book taught you about family?
- Did you like the book? Why? Why not?

Main activity 23

A book review

AFTER READING

⏱ **50** **Resources required:** access to the internet

• **Children should be able to:**

assess the effectiveness of their own and others' writing.

1. Ask children what a book review is and what its purpose is. Show some online reviews for *Boy in the Tower* and read some aloud. Ask children which points they agree with and which points they disagree with.

2. Model writing the answers to the following questions.
   - What is the book about?
   - What did you like about it?
   - What didn't you like about it?
   - Would you recommend the book? Why? Why not?

T Ask children to design a poster recommending the book.

D Ask children to write a succinct summary of the book for their review.

Children could write for a real purpose: a school newsletter or online publication.

Main activity 24

Poetry: *Bluchers* comparison

AFTER READING

⏱ **40** **Resources required:** photocopy master (PCM) 12

• **Children should be able to:**

summarise the main ideas drawn from more than one paragraph, identifying key details that support the main ideas; making comparisons within and across books.

1. Using the poem (PCM 12) and the text, discuss and collect adjectives to describe how Ade feels when he is trapped by the Bluchers in the tower. Encourage children to think of interesting adjectives that they don't use very often.

2. Display the question: In what way are the Bluchers like Ade's mum's illness?

3. Children write a series of sentences to answer this question. Model how to structure the sentences, using evidence from the text and the poem, e.g. 'The Bluchers trap people in their homes and Ade's mum's illness keeps her in the flat.'

T This activity is intended for children working at the 'towards level' but can be differentiated as shown.

S Children could write their answer in paragraphs.

D Children could answer the question: To what extent are the Bluchers and Ade's mum's illness alike? This will involve assessing how similar they are, and including ways in which they are different.

Main activity 25

Poetry: *Bluchers* art

Resources required: photocopy master (PCM) 12, watercolour paints, black paper, blue shiny paper, scissors, glue

- **Children should be able to:**

  improve their mastery of art and design techniques, including drawing, painting and sculpture, with a range of materials [for example, pencil, charcoal, paint, clay].

1 Using the poem (PCM 12) and the book, create a list of verbs and adjectives on the board to describe the appearance and movement of the Bluchers around the tower.
2 Using watercolours, children create a backdrop of the sky.
3 Using the black paper, children create a silhouette of the tower.
4 Using the blue shiny paper, children cut out and stick on the Bluchers around the tower.

T This activity is intended for children working at the 'towards level' but can be differentiated as shown.

S Children consider how to show perspective in the artwork.

D Children could write a short description of their method, the materials used and the effect achieved.

Main activity 26

Poetry: *Binley House* mini-project

2 x **Resources required:** photocopy masters (PCM) 11 and 13

- **Children should be able to:**
  describe settings, characters and atmosphere; discuss writing similar to that which they are planning to write in order to understand and learn from its structure, vocabulary and grammar.

1. In the first session, children use PCM 11 to collect the sights, sounds and smells described in the poem *Binley House* (PCM 13).

2. Encourage children to start to think of their own home and what sights, sounds and smells they encounter there. They could even think about the textures of things they touch and tastes of things that they often eat at home.

3. Children make a list of their observations for each sense. They could write single words or begin to construct poetic phrases of their own.

4. Children could illustrate their notes, as this often helps with further idea generation.

5. In the second session (or when they are ready), children write their own poems about where they live. They can choose to follow the structure of *Binley House* or use their own idea.

T Children focus on one sense. For example, if they have a busy home, they might focus on sounds: conversations, pets, the television and radio, etc.

S This activity is intended for children working at the 'securing level' but can be differentiated as shown.

D Children focus on building their ideas into similes and metaphors so that their poem is more abstract and less literal.

It would be useful to undertake Plenary activity 28 before the second session of this activity.

Main activities 27–28

Poetry: origami crane

2 × 30 **Resources required:** access to the internet, scrap paper, plain origami paper, coloured pencils

- **Children should be able to:**

   select from and use a wider range of tools and equipment to perform practical tasks [for example, cutting, shaping, joining and finishing], accurately.

1 In the first session, find an online video with simple instructions for how to make an origami crane. Watch it as a class.

2 Hand out some pieces of scrap paper so that children can practise making their cranes. Replay the video, pausing after each step to check whether children have followed it correctly. Make sure that you recycle any discarded attempts!

3 In the second session, children will make an origami crane that is decorated with their hopes. They start by writing their hopes on a piece of origami paper. It could be a hope for their future self or a hope for the world around them.

4 Children turn over the paper and decorate it with a pattern relevant to what they have written on the other side.

5 Replay the video, pausing as before after each step. Children follow the steps to create their crane, taking extra care with this final version.

6 Display the cranes in the classroom, or allow children to take them home.

> If children struggle to follow the video instructions, demonstrate the process yourself.

Main activities 29–30

Plenary activities

Famous towers

 **Resources required:** plain paper, coloured pencils, pictures of famous towers (T only)

- **Children should be able to:**
  make comparisons within and across books.

1 The title of the book suggests that a tower will be a key part of the story. Ask children to think of famous real towers or towers from stories that they know.
2 In groups, children note these down in different colours. One colour for real towers and one for fictional towers.

T Children could have picture prompts to help them think of famous towers.

D Ask children to think about what a tower might represent in stories (i.e. trapped, out of reach, high up, imprisoned).

Some real examples might include: Tower of London, Oxo Tower, Eiffel Tower, Leaning Tower of Pisa, Twin Towers, Grenfell Tower. Fictional towers might include towers from: Rapunzel, Sleeping Beauty, Rumpelstiltskin.

— **Plenary activity 1** —

Expanded nouns

 Vocabulary builder

- **Children should be able to:**
  use expanded noun phrases to convey complicated information concisely.

1 Children play this game in groups of three.
2 One child says the name of something you might see out of the window of a tower, e.g. houses.
3 The next child expands the noun by adding an adjective, e.g. miniscule houses.
4 The third child expands the noun using a prepositional phrase, e.g. miniscule houses along a street.
5 Children continue adding adjectives and prepositional phrases (seven miniscule terraced houses along a busy street) until someone forgets one of the descriptors.
6 Children repeat the game with a new noun, changing the person that starts.

— **Plenary activity 2** —

Bluchers evidence

 10

- **Children should be able to:**

   provide reasoned justifications for their views; draw inferences such as inferring characters' feelings, thoughts and motives from their actions, and justify inferences with evidence.

1 After reading pages 3–5, ask children to consider whether they think Bluchers are a good or bad thing to Ade.

2 Once established that Bluchers are a bad thing (although Ade finds them quite beautiful later in the book), children scan the text to find three words that support this judgement. Encourage children to choose vocabulary that strongly supports the view.

Plenary activity 3

Sketching Bluchers

15 **Resources required:** paper; drawing or painting materials

- **Children should be able to:**

   predict what might happen from details stated and implied.

   improve their mastery of art and design techniques, including drawing, painting and sculpture, with a range of materials [for example, pencil, charcoal, paint, clay].

1 After reading pages 3–5, ask children to create a quick drawing or painting of the Bluchers taking over a city.

2 Explain to the children that, as they don't have much description at this stage, their individual interpretations of something destructive and devastating may be very different.

You may want to display these and update and replace them as children learn more about what the Bluchers look like.

Plenary activity 4

You're a grown up now

- **Children should be able to:**

   understand what they read by checking that the book makes sense to them.

  punctuate bullet points consistently.

1 Ask children to read pages 19–23 independently.

2 Ade's mum says he is 'grown up now'. Ask children to write a bullet pointed list of the 'grown up' activities that he does in pages 19–23. The activities include: walking to school alone, getting money out of the cash point, going shopping, cooking dinner.

3 Remind children to punctuate their bullet points correctly.

D Children think about why Ade is being asked to do all these jobs: is it because his mum wants him to be 'grown up' or is there another reason?

Plenary activity 5

Lip-reading

- **Children should be able to:**

   understand that differences and similarities between people arise from a number of factors, including cultural, ethnic, racial and religious diversity, gender and disability.

1 Gaia has a skill for lip-reading. Allow children to have a go at reading lips. Mouth a sentence of your choice three times to the class. (You may want to link this to the text.)

2 Children write down what they think you are saying.

3 Discuss different interpretations and ask children to think about situations when lip-reading could be useful or cause problems.

4 Ask children to imagine that they cannot hear and can only read lips to understand what people are saying. What would they find particularly difficult about this?

Plenary activity 6

Headlines

READ UP TO PAGE 75

- **Children should be able to:**
  - summarise the main ideas drawn from more than one paragraph, identifying key details that support the main ideas.
  - use further organisational and presentational devices to structure text and to guide the reader [for example, headings, bullet points, underlining].

1. Discuss how a number of newsworthy things happen in pages 55–75.
2. Ask children to come up with a news headline to summarise the unusual happenings in each chapter.

Plenary activity 7

Scrapbook

DURING READING

3 × 10 **Resources required:** scrapbooks (or sheets of paper stapled into a booklet), coloured pencils, glue, newspapers, magazines

- **Children should be able to:**
  - check that the book makes sense to them, discussing their understanding; ask questions to improve their understanding.

1. On page 42, Ade mentions his scrapbook. He begins to collect information about the situation and what he knows about the Bluchers, continuing to do so as the story develops, i.e. page 120; page 142; page 274.
2. Give children their own scrapbooks in which to collect what they find out about Bluchers, using doodles, drawings, magazine cuttings, pictures, etc. If you need to, you could make scrapbooks by folding some sheets of paper in half to make a spine, before stapling along the spine.
3. At three (or more) points during the story, allow children to spend ten minutes filling in their scrapbooks with interesting words, images and plot points. Alternatively, children may want to have access to their scrapbooks throughout the whole reading process and update as and when they find out more.

T You could give children headings, which they could use to organise their information, e.g. Appearance, Likes, Dislikes.

D Children could research and collect real news stories that are relevant to add to their scrapbook.

Plenary activities 8–10

If I were …

3 × ⏱10

- **Children should be able to:**
  - articulate and justify answers, arguments and opinions; predict what might happen from details stated and implied.
  - recognise vocabulary and structures that are appropriate for formal speech and writing, including subjunctive forms.

1. At the following key points in the story, characters face dilemmas.
   - **Chapter Twenty-one:** Ade is watching residents leave the towerblocks, hoping that Gaia is among them. He can't see her from the window but doesn't have a phone to call her to check.
   - **Chapter Thirty-one:** Ade can see that Gaia's tower is under threat, and he and Ben decide to help.
   - **Chapter Forty-three:** Ade has decided to go outside to help the person he thinks he has seen. Obi and Ben are calling him back but he is determined to help.

   Children use the subjunctive sentence stem 'If I were …' to discuss what they would do if they were in that character's situation.

2. Children can write their ideas as sentences, using commas accurately: If I were Ade, I would run into the nearest building as quickly as possible.

   Children could be given two options for each dilemma and they could discuss which they would choose. Ask them to repeat their chosen sentence to practise using the subjunctive voice.

Plenary activities 11–13

Asking questions

READ UP TO PAGE **94**

⏱10

- **Children should be able to:**
  - ask questions to improve their understanding.

1. Take the role of the prime minister and offer to answer any questions that children (in role as members of the public) have about the situation.

2. In pairs, children think of three questions that they would like to ask.

3. Take the hot-seat with children asking their questions and you responding in character. Encourage children to ask challenging questions, such as: 'What measures are being put in place to ensure the Bluchers don't spread?' or 'Who is taking responsibility for this disaster?'

Plenary activity 14

What next?

Read up to page 169

- **Children should be able to:**
  predict what might happen from details stated and implied.

1. Ask children to imagine how Ade felt after Obi left the tower. Write key words on the board.
2. Children write the next paragraph, predicting what happens next. They could write from Ade's or Obi's point of view. Children can use the words on the board to inspire them.

T Allow children to write in whichever tense they prefer.

D Encourage children to write in the present tense and in the style of the author.

Plenary activity 15

True or false?

During reading

3 x

- **Children should be able to:**
  check that the book makes sense to them, discussing their understanding and exploring the meaning of words in context.

1. This activity can be carried out at various points during reading. Read out the following statements relating to the chapters you have read.
2. Children show their understanding of the text by either putting their thumbs up if a statement is true or down if a statement is false.

Pages 3–94:
- Ade's neighbour is called Michael.
- Ade lives on the 14th floor.
- The first building to fall is called The George.
- Ade lives with his mum.

Pages 95–222:
- Obi is the caretaker of the tower.
- Dory often cooks Ade dinner.
- Gaia's tower stays standing.
- The Bluchers eat grass.

Pages 223–329:
- Pigeon is a pigeon.
- Salt kills Bluchers.
- Dory saves the cat.
- All characters move to the seaside.

Plenary activities 16–18

Guess who?

 Resources required: sticky labels

- **Children should be able to:**
  provide reasoned justifications for their views; distinguish between statements of fact and opinion.

READ UP TO PAGE 222

1. Place a sticky label on the back of each child with a character's name on it.
2. Children walk around the room, asking one question to each person they encounter to try to find out which character they are. Questions should only have yes / no answers and they can't ask 'am I Ade?', for example.
3. Once they have guessed their character, they can give a simple opinion on that character, with reasons to justify their views.

T Encourage children to focus on appearance and the character's actions.

D Encourage children to focus on the character's motivation.

Plenary activity 19

Rollercoaster of emotions

3 x **Resources required:** paper, pencils

- **Children should be able to:**
  identify main ideas drawn from more than one paragraph and summarise these; draw inferences such as inferring characters' feelings, thoughts and motives from their actions, and justify inferences with evidence.

AFTER READING

1. This activity can be carried out at the end of three lessons, focussing on a different character each time. Model how to draw a 'rollercoaster' line on paper, annotating it with emotions of the character over time. You could choose to model with a character from the book, or draw a rollercoaster of your own day.
2. Children draw the rollercoaster lines of three of the key characters in the story: Ade, Ben and Dory.

   Encourage children to think about high points and low points first. For example, Ade's line would dip low when he is dehydrated but go up when he meets Dory and Obi. Remind children to use evidence from the text to back up their thoughts.

T You could give children rollercoaster lines that you have already drawn, and ask them to label the lines with key plot points.

D Children could draw two character's rollercoasters simultaneously on one piece of paper, showing interaction between the two, or annotate their rollercoasters with more complex feelings, such as jealousy, confusion and nervousness.

Plenary activities 20–22

Why?

Resources required: A3 paper

- **Children should be able to:**
  draw inferences such as inferring characters' feelings, thoughts and motives from their actions, and justify inferences with evidence.

1 Write the following questions on A3 paper and place one on each table.
  - Why doesn't Ade's mum leave the house?
  - Why do Dory and Obi stay in the tower?
  - Why did Ben stay in his tower?
  - Why do Gaia's family leave the area?
  - Why don't the characters get saved by the emergency services earlier?

2 Children move around the tables in groups, adding their answers to each question. If they agree or disagree with an answer already on the paper, they can add their own thoughts.

AFTER READING

Plenary activity 23

Non-fiction: safe zones

Resources required: atlases, photocopy master (PCM) 8 and 10, coloured pencils

- **Children should be able to:**
  name and locate counties and cities of the United Kingdom, geographical regions and their identifying human and physical characteristics; use maps, atlases, globes and digital / computer mapping to locate countries and describe features studied.

1 Ask children to read the text on PCM 8.
2 Ask them to use their atlases to locate London and Brighton, then mark them on the map on PCM 10.
3 Ade uses red crosses to show which buildings have fallen. Ask children to find an appropriate way to show the safe zones that are listed on PCM 8.

AFTER READING

Plenary activity 24

Poetry: *Bluchers* – active and passive

 Resources required: photocopy master (PCM) 12

- **Children should be able to:**
  use passive verbs to affect the presentation of information in a sentence.

1 Explain the difference between the passive voice (the subject is acted upon by the verb) and the active voice (the subject acts upon the verb).

2 Ask children to identify where the passive voice is used in the poem (PCM 12).

3 Model how to change it from the passive voice to the active voice, e.g. 'we are held in their clutches' becomes 'they hold us in their clutches'.

4 Children change the following sentences from passive to active voice.
- We are entangled in their arms.
- We are enslaved by them.
- We are imprisoned within the walls.

T This activity is intended for children working at the 'towards level' but can be differentiated as shown.

S Children could write their own passive sentences about the Bluchers. These can be swapped with a partner, who could turn them into the active voice.

D Ask children to consider why the poet has used the passive voice. (It could be to show that the people are powerless against the Bluchers or as a technique to make them seem more mysterious.)

Plenary activity 25

Poetry: *Bluchers* – hyphens

AFTER READING

⏱ **Resources required:** plain paper, pencils

- **Children should be able to:**
  -  ask questions to improve their understanding.
  - use hyphens to avoid ambiguity.

1 Display the following hyphenated words and discuss how the hyphens are used for clarity and to avoid ambiguity: a tower-eating Blucher; a brick-crushing Blucher; a sky-scraping building; a human-killing plant.

2 Children draw two sketches: one to represent the hyphenated phrase and one to represent the un-hyphenated phrase, e.g. a tower eating (a) Blucher and a tower-eating Blucher.

🅣 This activity is intended for children working at the 'towards level' but can be differentiated as shown.

🅢 Ask children to choose a phrase and explain briefly to a friend the difference in meaning between the hyphenated and un-hyphenated versions.

🅓 Ask children to come up with their own ambiguous phrases that can be clarified with hyphens. Encourage children to use grammatical terminology (noun; verb; adjective) to explain how the hyphen changes the meaning of the sentence.

Plenary activity 26

Poetry: *Binley House* questions

AFTER READING

⏱ **Resources required:** photocopy master (PCM) 13

- **Children should be able to:**
  - ask questions to improve their understanding.

1 Take the role of the poet Joseph Coelho and offer to answer any questions that children have about the poem (PCM 13).

2 Children note down three questions that they would like to ask the poet. Encourage children to write questions that are relevant to the poem.

3 Take the hot-seat as the poet, with children asking their questions. Respond in character.

🅣 Children think of one question each and share it with their neighbour. If their neighbour's questions sparks an idea for another, they can write that one down too.

🅢 This activity is intended for children working at the 'securing level' but can be differentiated as shown.

🅓 Children focus on questions that will bring out a personal opinion.

Plenary activity 27

Poetry: *Binley House* metaphors — AFTER READING

 Vocabulary builder Resources required: photocopy master (PCM) 13

- **Children should be able to:**

  know the technical and other terms needed for discussing what they hear and read, such as metaphor, simile, analogy, imagery, style and effect; discuss and evaluate how authors use language, including figurative language, considering the impact on the reader.

1 Ask: How does Joseph Coelho compare Binley House to a monster? Encourage verbal responses to the question, in which children should use examples of metaphors from the poem (PCM 13) to support their ideas.

2 Ask: Why does Joseph Coelho compare the tower to a monster?

T Remind children what a metaphor is, using examples as necessary.

S This activity is intended for children working at the 'securing level' but can be differentiated as shown.

D Ask children to choose the metaphor they feel is the most effective. Encourage them to explain how it is effective.

It may be useful to undertake this activity before children write their own poem in Main activity 28.

Plenary activity 28

Poetry: *Hope* by heart — AFTER READING

2 x **Resources required:** photocopy master (PCM) 14

- **Children should be able to:**

  learn a wider range of poetry by heart.

1 Across two sessions, give children time to learn part or all of the poem (PCM 14) by heart.

2 Children perform the poem to each other, evaluating effectiveness. Ask children to consider the punctuation in the poem and how this might be reflected in the way they perform it.

T Children could split into groups of three, learning one stanza each and performing as a group.

S Children could create cue cards with images on to remind them of the first line of each stanza. For example, they could draw a feather, a boiled sweet and an ear.

D This activity is intended for children working at the 'deeper level' but can be differentiated as shown.

Plenary activities 29–30

Making connections

PCM 1

The buildings kept falling
Ade's mum is unwell
Gaia is an excellent gardener
The children were worried
Ade grabbed the money from the cash point

;	;	;	;	;

she hasn't left the house in a long time.
her sunflower grew taller than all the rest.
they looked like they might cry at any minute.
no-one knew why they were collapsing.
he shoved the notes in his pocket and ran home.

© Pearson Education Ltd 2019   Pinpoint English Whole Class Reading Y6: Boy in the Tower

Ade's mum

PCM 2

Explain why you are writing a letter (rather than talking directly to her) and what you hope the letter will achieve.	
Explain what you are worried about.	
Explain what you think she should do.	
Finish by asking her some questions, telling her how much you care about her and saying again what you hope the letter will achieve.	

Best friends

PCM 3

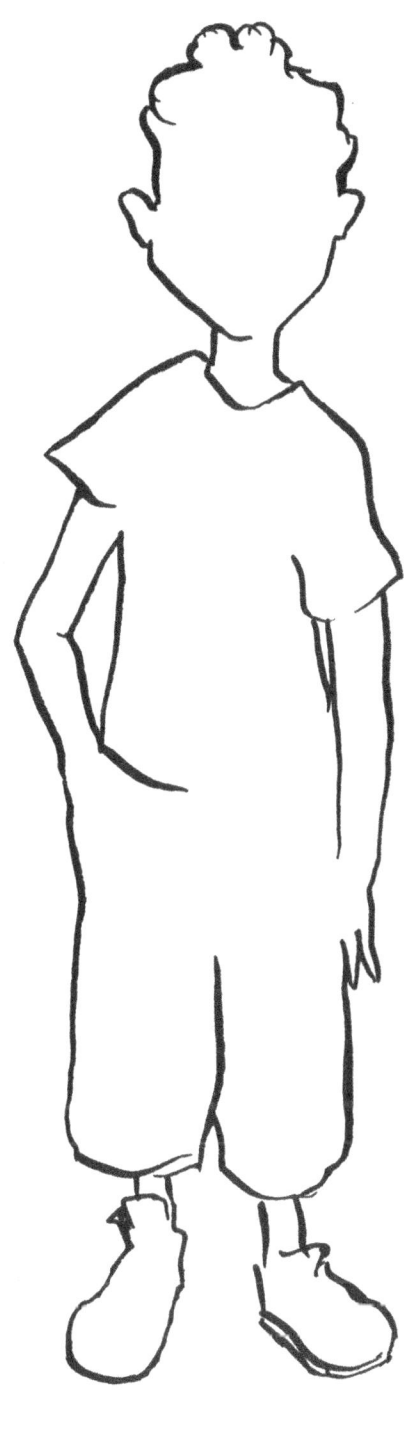

Discussion text

PCM 4

Title	Should Ade leave the tower?
Introduction Give the background information and tell the reader what you will be discussing.	
Arguments for Tell the reader why Ade should leave the tower.	
Arguments against Tell the reader why Ade should not leave the tower.	
Conclusion Make your mind up and tell the reader what you have decided.	

You can use conjunctions such as: whereas, although, however, on the other hand.

Adaptation explanation

How have carnivorous plants evolved and adapted to their environments?

Carnivorous plants grow wild all over the world, except in Antarctica. You will find them in coastal areas, and in marshes and mosslands, where many other plants would find it difficult to survive because of poor soil quality. Carnivorous plants have learned to adapt to these environments.

They get plenty of oxygen, water and sunshine, which helps them to grow and thrive. However, plants also need nitrogen and other minerals. Most plants get them from the soil in which they grow but carnivorous plants do not. This is because the soil in their usually warm, wet habitats doesn't contain a lot of nitrogen. Instead, these plants have found an alternative source of the gas – insects!

Carnivorous plants have adapted, in different ways, to attract, trap and digest insects to survive. For example, the Venus flytrap has a mouth-like trap that shuts very quickly, trapping insects inside, whereas sundews have sticky tentacles that suffocate their prey.

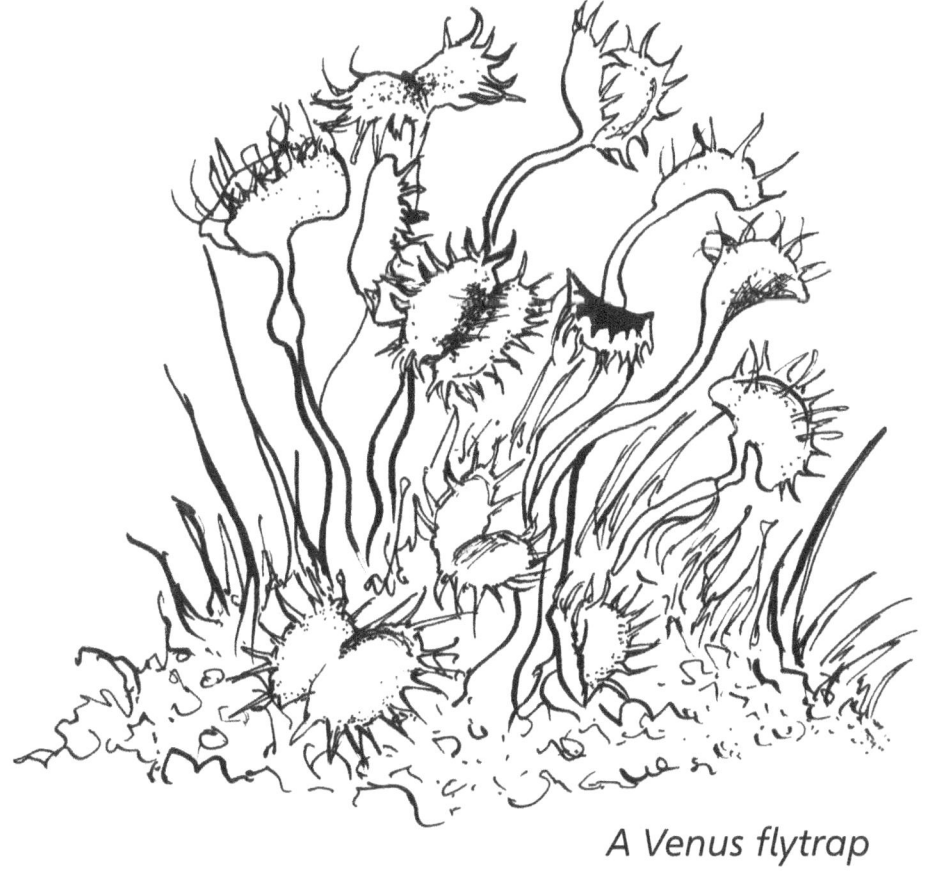

A Venus flytrap

New friends

PCM 6

The ending

PCM 7

The tower crashes down.

Ade cries.

Ade hears the sound of the helicopter.

Obi tapes Ade's mask to his face.

Obi saves Pigeon.

Ade and his mum go onto the roof.

Ade opens the door and leaves the tower.

Dory explains why she and Obi didn't leave the tower with everyone else.

Non-fiction text

URGENT PUBLIC HEALTH MESSAGE FROM THE GOVERNMENT

Dear resident,

As you are aware, your towerblock is located in what is known as a '**Blucher** Disaster Area' and is under severe **threat**. Please read the following information carefully and follow the advice herein.

What we know:

- The plants known as 'Bluchers' have been confirmed by scientists as a new **species**.
- The species is deadly and has already claimed over 200 buildings and 500 lives in your area.
- The Bluchers grow quickly and silently.
- They feed on concrete, glass and metal by releasing an **enzyme** that dissolves the materials.
- Bluchers also release **spores** into the air which are **poisonous** when breathed in by humans.

Safety guide:

- Where possible, residents are advised to leave the area immediately and head to an official **safe zone** on the coast. Your closest safe zones are: Southend-on-Sea, Brighton, Eastbourne, Margate and Whitstable.
- When you **vacate**, please ensure you cover your body completely and wear a mask.
- If you are not able to leave your home, stay inside at all times and wait for assistance.
- Do not touch the Bluchers under any circumstances.
- If you have come into contact with the Bluchers, do not touch any other member of your family or the public. Wash immediately and stay in **isolation** until further notice.

Please be assured that scientists, government officials and the emergency services are working to find a solution to this crisis.

We urge you to stay calm and support your neighbours.

Non-fiction: quick comprehension

PCM 9

Use the Blucher health message to answer these questions.

1. According to the text, how many buildings and lives have the Bluchers already claimed?

_____

_____

2. How do the Bluchers dissolve materials like concrete?

_____

_____

3. Why are spores dangerous?

_____

_____

4. What do you need to do when you leave your house?

_____

_____

5. What should you do if you touch a Blucher accidentally?

_____

_____

The question words (how many, how, why, what) will help you to work out how to answer the question.

Non-fiction: safe zones

PCM 10

Poetry: *Binley House* mini-project

PCM 11

	Sights	Smells	Sounds
Binley House			
My house			

Simile ideas	
Metaphor ideas	

Bluchers

Trapped and choked, we are held in their clutches.
Grasped tight and suffocating, we are entangled in their arms.

No air to breathe …
No room to move …

See how the beautiful blue
hides the bile beneath the Bluchers.

Enclosed and alone, we are enslaved by them.
Surrounded, we are imprisoned.

No air to breathe …
No room to move …

See how the beautiful blue
hides the bile beneath the Bluchers.

Annabel Gray

Binley House

TV aerials like dead branches,
satellite dishes like dead eyes,
rusted, but still they stared.
It was a zombie of a block.

The bin chute
made the mouth of the block.
Every day we fed it...

dinners left to go stone cold,
bags of clothes from missed fathers,
tissues soaked in tears.

The cold whistles of wind
from the corridors of Binley House
became the block's hiss for more.

The slam of distant doors
from the homes within Binley House
became the block's rumble of hunger.

We fed the block our lives:
the good times, the bad times,
evenings spent with friends who lived
above, below and side by side.

Gazing at stars from five storeys up,
smelling the bins from five storeys below.
Overheard arguments.
Overheard laughter.

We fed the block our lives
as it swelled
its monstrous city around us.

Joseph Coelho

Hope

Hope is the thing with feathers

That perches in the soul,

And sings the tune without the words,

And never stops at all,

And sweetest in the gale is heard;

And sore must be the storm

That could abash the little bird

That kept so many warm.

I've heard it in the chillest land,

And on the strangest sea,

Yet, never, in extremity,

It asked a crumb of me.

Emily Dickinson

Answers

PCM 1: Making connections

The buildings kept falling; no-one knew why they were collapsing.

Ade's mum is unwell; she hasn't left the house in a long time.

Gaia is an excellent gardener; her sunflower grew taller than all the rest.

The children were worried; they looked like they might cry at any minute.

Ade grabbed the money from the cash point; he shoved the notes in his pocket and ran home.

PCM 7: The ending

Dory explains why she and Obi didn't leave the tower with everyone else.

Ade cries.

Obi tapes Ade's mask to his face.

Ade opens the door and leaves the tower.

Ade hears the sound of the helicopter.

Ade and his mum go onto the roof.

Obi saves Pigeon.

The tower crashes down.

PCM 9: Non-fiction: quick comprehension

1. Over 200 buildings and 500 lives.
2. By releasing an enzyme that dissolves the materials.
3. They are poisonous when breathed in by humans.
4. Cover your body completely and wear a mask.
5. Do not touch anyone. Wash immediately and stay in isolation.

Notes